How I Saw It:
A Stroll Thro' Old Cardiff Bay

Harry "Shipmate" Cooke

with illustrations by Jack Sullivan

BUTETOWN HISTORY & ARTS CENTRE

Published by Butetown History & Arts Centre
5 Dock Chambers
Bute Street
Cardiff CF1 6AG

ISBN 1-898317-05-4

Copy Editing: Glenn Jordan, Molly Maher,
Chris Weedon & Philip Willcox

Cover Illustration: Jack Sullivan
Layout & Typesetting: Word Up Design

Art Reproduction: Athena Repro
Printed by: British Gas, Wales

A publication in the *Life Stories from Tiger Bay* Series.
Series Editor: Glenn Jordan
Associate Editor: Molly Maher

ROOTS

Cardiff my wonderful city,
you're all that a city should be;
with roots in the lilt of the valley,
your past is a song of the sea.

City of beauty and culture,
Empress of mountains and vales;
Cardiff my wonderful city,
Celtic maiden of Wales.

ACKNOWLEDGEMENTS

This book is dedicated to the folks of the Docks,
past and present.

Thanks to all of you who made this publication
possible, especially the staff of Butetown History
and Arts Centre and Jack Sullivan, who provided
the illustrations.

Kitbag in Hand

CONTENTS

CHAPTERS

I	The Docks and Solly Andrews	1
II	Masters and Mortals	19
III	Hardmen	35
IV	Big Windsor and the Latin Quarter	41
V	A James Street Jaunt	47
VI	Holy Days	53
VII	Larboard and the Boat People	59
VIII	Medicos and Moonlights	67
IX	Bay Ghosts	75
X	Bute Street Tapestry	85

Docklands Remembered

Sometimes I pause and think awhile,
as I sit in the corner chair,
of yesterday, the dockland scene,
of life and how we were.

New Year's Eve at the Pierhead,
the fun of Auld Lang Syne,
a multiracial symphony,
and the blood like vintage wine.

James Street in its heyday,
the world within our reach,
chops and chips and cabbages,
gas mantles four pence each.

The docks and diving cormorants,
and Solly Andrews' tea,
riggers, trimmers, tugboat men,
the pit props on the quay.

Ore for the Dowlais Steelworks,
ships about to sail,
coal dust dancing in the sun,
like a drunken widow's veil.

Steam trains shouting at the night,
a hissing metalled roar,
as they shunt screaming gulls awake,
on the strutting pigeoned shore.

Trawler men in pipe-smoked pubs,
and sailors homeward bound,
the merry, mad-capped, rushing docks,
a cacophony of sound.

Time is just a trollop,
who steals life's every page,
but the book of the Docklands' history,
is one it can't erase.

Chapter I

The Docks
and Solly Andrews

Home again from China seas
and the coast of Sarawak
I took a stroll down Cardiff Bay
my seabag on my back.

Stowin' my gear in Cory's Rest
I went out for a drink
and as I sat there in the snug
a lady tipped a wink.

Good day my jolly sailor boy
you're home at last from sea
you're bronzed and strong and full of fire
and handsome too, said she.

Come sit you down and stay awhile
and tell me sailors' tales
of Davy Jones and mermaids
of Neptune and the whales.

A widow woman, so she said
her husband drowned at sea
as she supped her gin, fluttered her eyes
and sang a song to me.

So I trimmed my sails and walked across
like any sailor would
then sat me down and ordered rum
and I knew she understood.

She kissed my cheek and with practised hands
ran her fingers through my hair
and spoke of a country cottage
that she and I could share.

But never trust the girls, me boy
they take us sailors in
as this so pretty filly did
when she slipped me a Micky Finn.

I woke up in the gutter
at the dawning of the day
and searching every pocket
I found she'd stolen all my pay.

So I signed aboard a tramp ship
and next time I come home
and dock again in Cardiff Bay
. . . I'll leave the girls alone.

Coming home

Jack Sullivan

4

I first shook hands with Cardiff as a boy seaman in the mid-thirties. Since those days I have walked every inch of the docklands a thousand times, from the foreshore to the Hayes. It was magic all those years back, and now, more than five decades later, it still is.

At first sight, the foreshore with its covering of brown mud looked like the surface of the moon, but this was far from the truth. The foreshore teemed with life. Crabs, eels, small and secret fish that would vanish as a shadow darkened their rock pool, and sea birds by the thousand. The sea birds are still there, walking about like hunched old men as they hunt for food, but the shellfish, once picked and eaten have gone; all that remains are untold thousands of empty shells lying atop the mud.

But even now the foreshore can still charm with its solitude, more so when the grey sea mist falls, and the lightship out in the channel barks its warning to mariners. Look closely, and some traces of the old foreshore remain. Barnacled bottle-tops sticking from the mud, part of an old steel plate from some long gone ship, and gnarled wooden posts that have stood there in the shard for a hundred years and more.

Years ago, mysterious men would hang fishing lines on the rope slung between the posts. Later, as the tide retreated, the men would return to retrieve the harvest of fish caught on the lines, and depart as silently as they came.

The docks proper, as I first knew them, have changed beyond recognition. Apart from the closure of the East and West Docks, the vitality that was once witnessed has gone.

The thirties dock was an everyday scene of activity— ships swinging at the buoys awaiting their turn for the coal hoists, riggers moving ships about, the better to load, and men in the ships' holds with huge shovels working to get the ships' trim right. As one vessel finished, so another came from the buoys to take its place. The coal hoists themselves were great steel spiders reaching eighty foot or more into the sky. They would snatch a twenty ton coal truck, twist it then turn it, before sending the contents roaring down a chute into the hold of a ship with a noise that sent the dock pigeons flying in fright.

At the close of the working day the hustle and bustle would diminish, but the dockland symphony would never cease entirely. The evening tide was always a signal for the Dowlais Steel Works to start. Vats of white-hot steel dross from the furnaces were trundled along the rail on the foreshore high bank, ready for tipping into the running tide. The meeting of boiling slag and cold sea water would be heard over half the city of Cardiff and the crimson glow that lit the night sky would be seen as far away as the Somerset coast. Local people—used to the sound through the years—ignored this, but this noise, plus the sight of screaming birds aroused from their roost, their shadows enhanced by the boiling clouds of steam, would send a stranger home to hide beneath the bedcovers.

But it was not all noise. One silent part of the dock housed three Spanish ships seeking refuge from the Spanish Civil War. They had lain at their berth in Cardiff for so long that sea grass and barnacles had taken hold of their underwater plates, and a passing ship's swell would reveal a marine growth akin to a coral reef.

Two of the sights missing now, that were prevalent in inter-war years, are the many bicycles and the moustaches of the dock hierarchy. From a dock foreman upward it seemed there was a pecking order among the top table—the higher up the ladder, the bigger the moustache— and no decent manager or superintendent would be seen out and about without a bowler hat. Every dock worker, it seemed, had a bicycle, splendid upright BSAs and others. They would be seen leaning together at the work place parked outside the dock cafés and taverns, and at the close of day, hundreds of men would swarm from the dock gate like a hive emptying of its bees.

The very first Cardiffian I became acquainted with was the seamen's bag man, Tich Cummings. Tich was a wonderful little man who had all the knowledge of the dock at his fingertips. One of his gifts was an instinctive know-how of every ship in the dock, and its every movement. He knew, before most, if a ship was to pay off its crew members, and he would always appear with his horse and cart at just the right moment like some genie. All seamen trusted Tich implicitly. They knew that once a bag was given into his charge, no matter what state they got into in some dockside tavern, the luggage would be as safe as the Bank of England, in the railway station awaiting their arrival. Two shillings was the fee for this service, plus his return fare bearing the claim slip from the station office. Other services were available too, services that were perhaps not quite what the authorities would have approved of. But they were gratefully accepted none the less. A slight nod of the head, plus an extra shilling, would ensure that a seaman's bag was placed at the bottom of the pile of luggage, and many an odd plug of tobacco or carton of cigarettes escaped the dry eye of the revenue men in this way. Tich did his job come rain or shine and, it was said that if the Devil were to ask Tich to look for his bags, they would be at the gates of hell when the Devil returned.

Sailor Man

I'm a hard case shell-back sailor man,
born in old Tiger Bay,
I've fought and drunk in every bar,
from there to Mandalay.

My daddy was an Irishman,
and he was a sailor too,
he pulled an octopus inside out,
off the coast of Wallamaroo.

My brother was a bully mate,
who spent his days in sail,
he went overboard off Lundy Isle,
and was swallowed by a whale.

And sometimes on a cloudy night,
he comes back from the dead,
to slither up the anchor chain,
and haunt the fo'c'sle head.

I've sailed with the sharks and dolphins,
and danced with a mermaid as well,
been frozen by ice in the Arctic,
and burned by the wild winds of hell.

And the day that I finish my roaming,
there's only one place I shall lay,
snugged sweet with the winkles and cockles,
down there in old Cardiff Bay.

Away from the larger docks, on the way to the dock gate stood Solly Andrews' café, and whilst there were, of course, other dock cafés, Solly's was the most frequented. The windows of Solly's were always painted half-way up in green paint. The front of the building was covered in enamelled wall signs advertising Fry's chocolate, Vimto and Players Navy Cut. And, of course, there were bicycles stacked along the wall awaiting their owners.

Inside the café the air was ever filled with the smell of stewed tea, and the sound of steel-studded boots that crunched on the coal gritted red tiled flooring. On the café's marbled counter, large aluminium hot-water boilers stood, gently steaming, as they awaited the call of the busy teapots which, once filled, always made a loud click as their lids snapped shut. Solly's was a place full of the conversation of dockers, elbows on the tables as they supped tea from thick mugs. Seamen in Libro dungarees, talked among themselves of voyages just completed, of voyages to come, of rounding Sydney Heads, New York and other places. Solly's was all this and more, it was a place of wonder for any small boy with a hint of salt in his veins who had slipped past the eye of the dock policeman and crept in to listen.

Walking from the café, the faint smell of fish and the sight of screaming, whirling sea birds would open another chapter in dock life. Cardiff's very own fleet of Neale and West deep-water fishing boats. In later years, after the Second World War, Neale and West were to close down their business after a seventy year association with Cardiff. The reason stated, was that the Welsh fishing grounds were depleted and the ships had to travel further for the catch. This, with the extra fuel required, meant higher cost. But the most damning report, which led to their departure, was of crew misbehaviour. There was crew trouble indeed. Trawler hands, if the catch were good, were much better paid than their brothers in deep-water service and whilst many of the fishermen were sober, family men, others were a wild bunch to say the least. Once ashore, their arrival at one of their favourite taverns was often a guarantee of mayhem with scenes akin to the old days on the Barbary Coast.

I remember inadvertently entering the Bridge Hotel in Bute Street one evening when a trawler had just docked. It was a scene that Hogarth would have been quite at home with: the wooden bar was awash with spilled ale, the landlord, shirt sticking to his back with the exertion of pulling endless pints of beer, barmaids dashing about with meat pies and plates of pickles and cheese. A few ladies sat at the bar, faces flushed with gin, whilst men pushed and pulled as they fought to get their pint pots refilled. Two or three drunks, open-mouthed and snoring, lay on the long bench by the wall, oblivious to the mayhem about them. And a piano player, hastily recruited, thumped away in a vain effort to drown the sound of Bing Crosby singing on the gramophone. But, best of all, a couple of wide-eyed men stomped up and down the bar, dancing a dance of their own design. Above it all a faint smell of fish, sweat and humanity, the whole mixed in a dense cloud of tobacco smoke.

Some of the characters that abounded in the atmosphere of the trawlers were pure Damon Runyan. There was a bow-legged Scot, no more than five foot tall who was known as "Bandy Jock." A kindly man when sober and a man who, if asked, could recite whole pages of the good book. Once the demon drink took over Jock, however, Hyde took over his Doctor Jekyll. Once when Jock was "steamed up" (to use his own words), he had but two ambitions, the first being to drink whatever hostelry he landed in dry, the second was to beat to a pulp any man taller than himself. Given Jock's size this meant he was at constant war with half the world's male population and the bold little man was never known to come aboard ship after a night ashore without at least one black eye.

There were able men who went to sea as cooks on the trawlers, some not so able. Most deep-water cooks would recoil in horror at the very thought of serving food in a ship's galley on a craft so small as to make cooking an abomination, the more so in foul weather when a heavy sea would seem to have these little ships standing on their beam ends. But all that was asked, and given, was a full belly—and gourmet meals they were not. Trawler men were noted for bestowing nicknames and one cook rejoiced in a name that spoke volumes about his culinary expertise. He was named "Bread 'n' Butter Sam."

But king of the dockside proper was, without doubt, the mighty railway engine. They were great steel monsters full of fire and steam who demanded right of way with many a shriek as they moved wagons of coal, steel and pit props, attached to them like a squealing umbilical cord. Pit props lay everywhere. Mountains of them on the quay sides and thousands of them sticking out of the clone-like rail trucks that stood awaiting removal to the coal mines in the Welsh valleys.

A shipmate of mine had first-hand knowledge of the same trucks of pit props. One evening, after a night ashore, he lost his way back to the ship and, befuddled with drink, he decided to sleep it off in a rail truck. In the early hours he was rudely awoken by the truck being shunted, and he leapt onto the dockside in terror, only to find he had removed his shoes and socks whilst in the truck and was standing on the cold dockside in his bare feet. Watching in dismay as the truck, plus his footwear, moved up the line, he said a silent prayer of thanks as he realised that the train had only moved the trucks onto another line. Hobbling over to retrieve his treasured shoes and socks, he suddenly realised every truck was a clone of its neighbour and a search would, to say the least, be futile. There was no alternative; he had to walk a couple of miles back to the ship, over coal-dusted roads in his bare feet, to the delight of the rest of the crew and an appreciative audience of cheering dock workers.

Like most ports, Cardiff had its quota of characters and sweet-talkers with an eye for a quick buck. "Bright Walter" was one such, a man with a beguiling manner and a tongue of pure silver that would charm a bunion off your foot. One wartime Christmas he sold a "pup" or rather a turkey, to a worldly wise Cockney docker, who was on loan from London to the Port of Cardiff and thought that anyone born outside the sound of Bow Bells was a village idiot. The docker just couldn't believe his luck. Food was on ration and poultry was just unheard of and here he was in possession, of all things, a turkey. Returning to his lodgings in triumph he presented the festive bird to his admiring landlady who, opening the bag with the turkey neck and head hanging from it, found inside a large house brick, wrapped carefully in layers and layers of newspaper. It was never known if Bright Walter's and the docker's paths ever crossed again.

Tommy, the dark-haired Irishman, ever the quick one, knew the gods were smiling on him when a group of Chinese seamen stopped him to enquire about clothing coupons. Once again, this was during the war. Tommy told the seaman that clothing coupons had to be purchased and, with the agreement of the seaman, he walked across the road to the post office. There he bought three hundred halfpenny stamps, returning to sell the stamps to his victims at half-a-crown each. Tommy was missing from his usual haunts for a while after this coup—probably a very wise move. There seemed a large number of irate Chinamen abroad, looking for someone, until their ship finally sailed.

Bert was a well-dressed little man, who could be found most afternoons with his half-pint of bitter in the lounge of the Mount Stuart Hotel. A loner, but pleasant enough to give you the time of day, Bert was well thought of, if only because of the rumour he had once done a stretch in Dartmoor prison. One day, armed with a large tape measure, he boarded a freshly docked ship, knocked the first officer's cabin door, informed the mate that he was the "super" and wished to take measurements of the alleyway for repairs, and asked would the mate please assist him. The mate was somewhat bemused, but agreed to help and Bert walked him around a corner in the alleyway, gave him the tape measure to hold whilst he took the other end and walked away. After a short while, the mate, growing impatient, peeped back around the corner to find the other end of the tape tied to his cabin door. Rushing back he found clothes, sextant, money and other valuables gone with the bogus "super." Bert was such a quiet man that his absence wasn't noticed in the lounge bar of the hotel for some considerable time. A few people showed some small interest but none more than various plain clothes detectives who came around quite often, but Bert was never seen again in the port of Cardiff.

Chapter II

Masters and Mortals

The Last Tramp Steamer

Sad old ship at the dockside,
awaiting the turn of the tide,
dark water and jostling flotsam,
chuckling and kissing your side.

The tugs will come in from the darkness,
and weep as they tow you away,
on your last acrimonious passage,
to the fires of the shipbreakers' bay.

Once you danced on the wide open sea lanes,
a gypsy, a lady for all,
the dolphins and sea wrack companions,
when your home was the next port of call.

Remember the green glow of phosphorus
on a bow waved warm tropic night,
the wonderful wild roaring forties,
when you fought the storm at its height.

The scent of the spices off Java,
a frigate birds cry to the moon,
the sound of the anchor chain surging,
when we stayed in that crystal lagoon.

No requiem plays at your passing,
no friend there to bid you goodbye,
who knows that the sea birds are grieving,
and perhaps a fool such as I.

L eaving the dock proper you came to the gates, which were ever manned by dock policemen. Their main tasks, it seemed, were to stop ladies slinking on to the ships or to leap out on unfortunate dock-workers, carrying home firewood taken from the dockside. Bute Place, the small street leading from the gates, housed the Seamen's Mission, Mount Stuart Hotel, the Post Office, the Mercantile Marine Office, the Seamen's Union and Silver's, the marine tailors. Silver's was a shop to command respect with its hawk-faced dummies, strategically placed in the window, each dummy dressed in blue serge officer's uniform with splendid peaked caps gazing out imperiously at the passers-by. The whole window was packed with items of nautical interest: cooks' checked trousers, black bridge coats, Libro dungarees, sheath knives, compass cards and woolly hats that some folk fondly thought jolly sailormen wore when dancing the hornpipe.

The Flying Angel Mission to Seamen was a grand old

building. Warm and cosy, with a billiard table, a small canteen serving tea and Oxo at a penny a cup, and an ever burning flame to light a man's cigarette on the counter. Once a month or so, during the winter, the Mission Padre organised a night of entertainment for out-of-work seamen. It never varied. There was a magician, and a conjurer, followed by a magic lantern show of the Rocky Mountains in winter or Travellers' Tales in the Sudan. Tea and rock cakes would be served during the interval by large, jolly ladies but most of the fun came from the magic lantern. The old chap who operated the magic lantern had failing sight and sometimes during the evening he would place a slide upside down. This would be greeted with screams of delight and during the confusion as he tried to get his act together, men would put their hands in the white beam of the lantern, to project lewd shadows onto the screen. The Padre would then flick on the house lights, glare at us all with a shocked expression, but I have a sneaking suspicion that he and his jolly ladies enjoyed the fun as much as the other rascals.

The Seamen's Union filled the corner of Bute Place and Bute Street and even there a discrimination showed through: firemen and sailors entered through one door, cooks and stewards through the other. On the other side of the street from the Seamen's Union stood the imposing block which housed the Docks Post Office with Paddy Usher's newspaper stand outside. Paddy was a "one off"—and a character in his own right. He had to be, peddling newspapers from an open pitch on the corner of a street where the east wind itself lived. He used large polished stones to anchor the news sheets against the elements, and, behind those twinkling blue eyes he had a secret few knew of. Paddy was an unofficial racing tipster. Every evening, with the help of a child's printing set and the following day's racing fixtures, our entrepreneur would print the names of horses on slips of paper and seal them in small envelopes. Gullible punters, out to make a fortune, bought these so called "Captain's Naps" as fast as the bold Paddy could print them and, who knows, Paddy's (or rather the Captain's) tips may have been more profitable than other so-called "hot shots," sent out by shady racing circles.

Next to the post office stood that holy of holies to all sailor men, the Mercantile Marine or Shipping Office. To the side of the great oaken doors that guarded the entrance to the Shipping Office stood an ornate Victorian drinking fountain, later to be removed to a Cardiff park where it now stands in all its glory. Ship Lane, the back entrance to the Shipping Office, was the entrance for the lower deck crowd. Officers used the front entrance to gain access to the inner sanctum and woe betide any poor galley boy found lurking near the hallowed frontage of the front office. Once inside the Shipping Office—a bleak, chairless mausoleum with yellowed walls and high, flyblown ceiling—one was in the lair of the Shipping Master, a man who, in his own estimation, must surely sit on the right hand of God.

Shipping Masters were a breed alone. Outside their official duties they were probably just ordinary "Johns," wife beaters, drunkards or saints, but once inside their sanctum, they were not as lesser mortals. Their very presence on arriving behind the polished counter, a single glance or raised eyebrow, would shrivel a master mariner or noisy crew to nail-biting silence. I knew one such. A portly fellow with a soft Irish accent who would look down his rum-veined nose and literally cause the hair on the nape of one's neck to tingle. This paragon, once reading out a Ship's Articles, paused, rested his eye on a long-haired prospective cabin boy and declared, "I'll not sign that youth until he gets his hair cut." The mate of the ship hastily passed a shilling to the shrinking lad, hissing that he should rush to the barbers and return before the crew finished signing Articles. The boy departed quickly from the accusing stare of the Shipping

Master, returning in next to no time looking like a shorn sheep.

It was in Cardiff's Shipping Office I saw the redoubtable Captain Jack, a man with such an evil reputation as to send shivers down the spine of any God-fearing sailor man. Captain Jack was, by all accounts, the terror of the seven seas, and a direct descendant of the old bully mates of the sailing ship era. Once at sea the bonny Captain would brook no deviation from his own code of behaviour and, at the first lapse, would take the offender to his cabin to be fined and have his name entered into the ship's log. Culprits could forego the fine if they cared to don boxing gloves and have a couple of rounds with the Captain on the bunker hatch. This challenge was often taken by men who thought they could gain the admiration of the rest of the crew by taking Captain Jack down a peg or two, but the Captain was ever the victor. The legends and fables that surrounded his stormy life abounded. They even included the manner of his death. It was said he was found with a knife between his ribs in a dark back alley in Shanghai and this rumour persisted for years. Whilst it was more than likely that the old man passed away peacefully in his own bed, this legend is, in a way, romantic, perhaps fitting to his image.

Challenge accepted

Let me say a small word about another legend—that of the mythical "Penniless Point"—before we leave the small Bute Place. The original Penniless Point in the 1930s was on the corner of Bute Street and Bute Place. The nickname was doubtless coined by some long gone wit, because it was the meeting place of out-of-work seamen who were looking for a berth, waiting for the pubs to open or just meeting old shipmates and friends. They would usually gather on the corner around ten o'clock each morning to tell yarns of subjects dear to the heart of deep-water men—of ships and trips and bumboat men, of storms and nights ashore. Noon or thereabouts they would disperse for a beer, to their homes, or perhaps for a walk about the dock to view future prospects.

In later years lesser mortals pontificated to newspapers about the whereabouts of this maritime speakers' corner and, in some mysterious way, nearly every other corner in Cardiff's docklands has been dubbed Penniless Point. But, for all that, the brooding shape of the Shipping Office was ever at the back of most onshore seafarers' minds. The Shipping Office was the provider of work, travel, food (of a kind) and instant cash, in the shape of an advance note against future earnings. Signing on a ship to obtain this advance in Cardiff Shipping Office

Signing on

was to come to grips with tradition. It was a sort of high mass that never, but never, changed. The Shipping Master would enter the room, walk slowly to the counter and gaze around at the assembled crew. Then, in the manner of the parish priest bestowing a benediction, he would reverently lift the ship's Articles from the counter. In the heavy silence to which this act gave rise, he would read the Articles. This done, the men would line up, sign Articles and usually ask for the prized advance on wages. This was given in the form of a note advising that the note might be cashed, but only when the ship had seen three days at sea. Thus the note was worthless in itself, but once outside the Shipping Office, the men would make a beeline for the waiting seamen's note casher— more often than not, Uncle Ike.

Uncle Ike was perhaps Cardiff's best known note casher and, what is more, he was a man of integrity. He would give the man the cash stated on the note, less two shillings in the pound in payment for the transactions. Not a princely sum even in those days because, should a man fail to sail on the ship, Ike would lose his money. This, however, seldom happened and, if Ike could cash twenty such notes each day for a week, it was a fair living. Uncle Ike had another string to his bow: he had a seamen's boarding house in Tiger Bay and reports said it was a well-run establishment.

The Docks was not just a place of railway trains, ships and coal. The Docks consisted of people, streets, houses and cats sleeping in the sun on backyard walls. The Docks meant neighbours and families and the good things in life. It was an exhilarating place to live in, and many of the menfolk who lived there worked in industries other than in the docks. As with other ports, the comings and goings, the sound of sea traffic, and shipping papers on view in most newsagents made the thought of far away places very real.

On Stuart Street, the nearest street to the waterfront, was the entrance to the Mountstuart Dry Docks with the noise of rivet guns, tugs sounding and sea birds screaming as its backdrop. On one side of the street there were houses and small shops with windows looking out. Among these was a double fronted window advertising "Bulwark Tobacco," "Digger Flake" and "Thick Twist" while hiding the barber's shop inside. The barber, an old gentleman, would surprise a new client by asking how he wished his hair cut—a rarity indeed in days when some barbers would advance and attack the chair-bound victim with ferocity. The bane of the old chap's life was his bald "plate." Outside in the street he would wear an ancient black beret. Inside the shop, at work, he wore a wig of alarming red hair that was never quite in place and would send customers into paroxysms of glee as he approached the chair with his red thatch at a very raffish angle.

Across the street from this tonsorial palace stood Campbell's Boat Yard. Discontinued during the war, 1946 saw the return of these small pleasure steamers, their coming as much a foretaste of the summer as the first cuckoo. Never shy of announcing their arrival, the pleasure boats would blast their steam whistles when at the outer reach bouys in the Cardiff approaches, to be answered by dredgers, tugs and deep-water Klaxons who would welcome their smaller sisters with delight.

Housewives would nod happily at the noise, children wiggle their toes, and the menfolk, whilst pretending to be unimpressed, smile in secret delight into their beer-pots. Campbell's navy was as much a part of Cardiff's maritime history as other and larger vessels. Better still, Campbell's arrival signalled the start of happy holidays.

Nonsense

We sailed one day on a marzipan boat
with liquorice sticks for our sails
the mast was made of cinnamon rock
the cargo was coconut snails.

When we finally reached the end of the world
a prawn asked the crew to have tea
and invited us all to the cuttlefish ball
in a cave at the bottom of the sea.

There were oysters, shrimps and jellyfish
ten lobsters hand in hand
fiddler crabs and young sand dabs
all dancing away to the band.

The piano and the harpsichord
were played by two blue whales
and a shark played solo trumpet
in a tall top hat and tails.

An octopus who blew a silver kazoo
played the drums and the bagpipes as well
whilst a walrus with a splendid moustache
beat time on an old ship's bell.

But we couldn't stay so we all sailed away
it was nearly time for our bed
and much too late for supper, of course
so we ate up our boat instead.

The Tale of Winnie the Winkle

Long long ago
on the edge of the sea,
a tiger shark said,
"Will you please marry me?"

To a young lady winkle
who was just swimming by,
a hat in her right hand,
a patch on her eye.

"Oh yes sir,"she said,
"and if I may say,
I've loved you quite madly
since Michaelmas Day."

The whelks and the oysters
danced in delight,
and said they should marry
that very same night.

Then a middle aged walrus
who lived in Cape Cod,
said "Really my dear,
it sounds rather odd."

But Old Father Neptune
said it was good,
if they wanted to wed,
and they could, well they should.

They were married next day
by a tortoiseshell cat,
in white leather breeches
and a red beaver hat.

Then they flew into space
on a silver balloon,
holding hands tight
for a long honeymoon.

And when they returned
to the edge of the sea,
the shark had the winkle
on toast for his tea.

Chapter III

Hardmen

Tussle in the tavern

The waterfront areas of all the world's ports were always viewed with suspicion by folk living in other districts. Stories of shadowy figures lurking on dark corners, flashing knives and other evils were ever the norm—most of these tall tales springing from the imagination of the press and others.

Dockland Cardiff was remarkably law-abiding, as many a drunken sailor man, staggering midnight streets unmolested, would doubtless agree.

An occasional redneck, ashore for a night on the tiles, caused trouble at times, but this was usually dealt with. The old adage "If you look for trouble, you'll get it" worked well, and not a few seamen returned to their ships chastened after a spanking by local men, irate at having their evenings spoiled in a local pub. But again, as in other ports, a tough area will ever throw up the tough guys, home-bred and otherwise. And Cardiff had its full share of the hard men. . . .

Mike, nicknamed "The Quiet Man," was one such. Never the man to court touble, his nickname was bestowed because of his soft manner of speech, but, for all that, each of his hands carried the kick of a mule.

Mike was as hard as they came. Before sailing the seas, he served a stint in the Irish Army and was an amateur boxing champion, once trained by an American heavyweight prize fighter.

Once challenged, against his will, to a fight in a dockside tavern, Mike sent his opponent packing after knocking him down three times, before returning to the bar to finish his drink. . . .

Later in the evening, Mike became most upset. Not because of the disturbance, not because of the fight, but because he'd discovered that during the affray he had lost a button from his new double-breasted coat.

Eddy D. was another such. A tall red-haired able seaman, Eddy was as tough as a teak, strong as a bull, and well known as one tough cookie.

Again, like "The Quiet Man," Eddy avoided trouble like the plague but, as usual, there was always some fool out to prove himself—an act that invariably ended in disaster for the challenger, because once aroused, Eddy had the mannerisms of a pitbull and could empty a saloon bar in seconds.

Eddy was a proud man and the very essence of the macho male, but he had a dark secret few knew of, and those who did wouldn't dare say.

Because of his physique, Eddy was very much in demand and sometimes whilst on shore leave he had a nice little earner—posing as an artist's model.

Another man, George, was of a much different calibre.

A hard man among hard men, he made his mark in dockland history and, even today, the old ones speak of him in awe.

Blessed with a barrel chest, his ginger hair wisped around a balding, domed head—a head used for his party piece, the "Liverpool kiss" or head-butt.

Such was this roaring boyo's reputation. It was known that his entrance into a public house would cause men to sup up their ale and depart the scene, quickly and silently.

Some of his encounters were legendary. Pub brawls, street fights, the lot. And many the young bucko feeling his feet had cause to regret a close encounter with George's bony skull. Once started there was no stopping this fellow. Seemingly impervious to pain, he would shake off blows to the head and body until closing on a victim he would butt him to sleep like a billy goat.

It is said that after an argument George once chased a man from a bar into the street, then finding the man had vanished, his rage was such that he ran over to a horse tethered to a cart and head–butted the animal, bringing the poor beast to its knees. . . .

In later years, deserted by sycophants who had dwelt in his shadow, George left Cardiff for good, and the last word on this broth of a boy was that he had taken his own life in London's Whitechapel.

There were others, many other hard cases. Some are long gone, others sleep their twilight years away in the sun on park benches as people past them by.

If they only knew, if they only knew. . . .

Chapter IV

Big Windsor
and the Latin Quarter

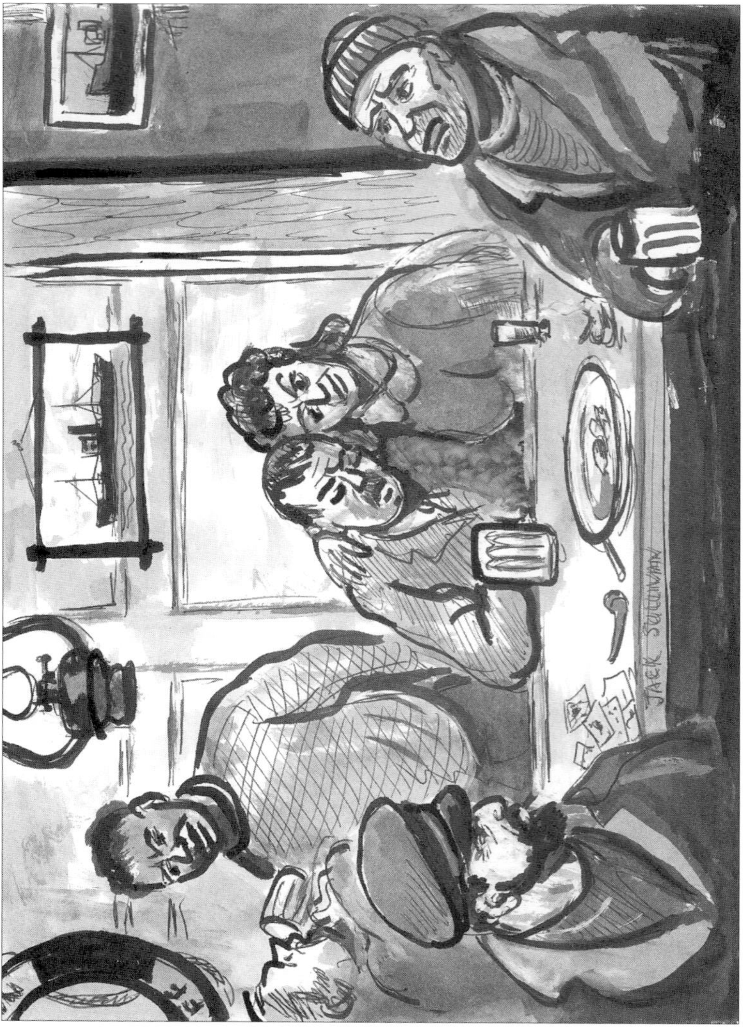

Love in the Snake Pit

On then, down Stuart Street past the Pilotage Office (now a listed building) to the Windsor Hotel. The "Big Windsor," standing as near the waterfront as possible was, in the war years, presided over by a French lady known by all as "Madame." She served a cordon bleu cuisine that drew gourmets from every walk of life. One could sit in the saloon bar and rub shoulders with film personalities, barristers, lords and their ladies. Yet just a few short yards from this most elegant of company stood the "snake pit" or public bar. Once inside the "snake pit" door and it was back to the last century. A sawdusted floor, spitoons and a large, open, coal fire. Maybe there was a gentleman sipping his whisky in one corner, in the other an old woman sniffing her snuff over her twopenny half-pint of scrumpy. The toilet arrangements in the snake pit were a little primitive, perhaps. There was just the one toilet, an evil box-like room with a solitary lightbulb hanging from flex in the ceiling, like an ever-open eye. Inevitably during an evening's session a lady would march to the toilet, after giving the potman stern command to keep a weather eye on the door whilst she was inside. Inevitably, the potman would forget and some poor unsuspecting drunk would lurch loo-ward. The resulting screams from the outraged "beldame" inside caused consternation in the bar and the bewildered drunk would be thrown into the street by the lady's friends. The snake pit has gone as have most of the people who lived its history. People like "Snuffy Jessie," "Toe-the-line Folley" and the "Dolly Sisters"—grand folk all, who could have walked the pages of a Dickens novel with ease.

The old Sailors' Home, next to the Big Windsor Hotel, was a large forbidding building, looking somewhat like a dilapidated warehouse. The rooms inside were like monks' cells, lit at one time by a solitary candle, and used mostly by old retired seamen who would sit outside come summer, their grey heads nodding in sleep in the warm sunshine. But the five streets—George Street, Louisa Street, South William Street, Adelaide Street and Evelyn Street—that linked Stuart Street to the Docks shopping centre, James Street, were far from sleepy. They contained the terraced houses of the Docks families, whose roots stretched back for generations, corner shops, a jobbing builder, a sail maker, bakers and Cardiff's own Latin quarter, George Street.

George Street's red-bricked library had two lady assistants and a large white cat who not only kept the mice at bay, but would sit on the counter, look at the borrower, then look at the books as if he had read them himself during the night hours. Of the small shops such as Isadoro's and Lewis's fresh fish, Josephina Perez was without doubt, a prince of general stores. "Joseys"—the memory of that little general store, even today, brings a far-away look into the old people's eyes. The smell of fresh baking bread, chrorizos, beans, peanuts and *cocido* stew cooking on the family stove, combined in a dance of delight that tingled the taste buds and would have tested the Baptist in the wilderness. She sold salt fish that was fit for a king, thick and white with grains of salt glittering like small diamonds. Now, long years since, people swear it has never been surpassed. Josey cooked her salt fish and called it *"bacalao"*—a dream of a dish with olive oil, garlic, onions and herbs. When the source of this delectable fish came to an end, Josey refused point blank to sell any other.

George Street's close neighbour, Louisa Street (again in the Latin Quarter) hosted two well-known Docks landmarks. The North and South, a small, comfortable tavern blessed with gossiping coal fires that gave a handshake on wintered evenings, and Tylkie's Barber Shop. Tylkie's small shop window was awash with marine bric-a-brac. Ship paintings, ship models, ships in bottles, the whole window spoke of the sea and would stop a passing stranger in his tracks at the sheer wonder of it all. Inside the shop itself one would be overcome with the heavy scent of hair oils, of unguents and pomades, and yet another display of ship models and old-world shaving mugs—truly a sight that would send today's collectors into ecstasies. The old streets are long gone. Pulled down to make a new generation of habitats but, in some way, the ghosts of small, white-limed back yards, the hint of a voice from a vanished tavern, a thought of small iron lampposts still prevail in the mind's eye.

Chapter V

James Street Jaunt

James Street Gone

Could I but turn a single page
in dockland's history book
and walk back into long ago
for one brief precious look.

Then from some shadowed vantage point
in secret yesterday
I'd watch the sherbert children dance
in hopscotch shouting play.

And pavements loud in people then
who gossip'd corner shops
that smell of soap and turpentine
of spice and lollypops.

Taverns filled with travellers tales
adventure and the sea
would lift the hem of days gone by
that nudge the memory.

As twilight brought the migrant moths
to flirt the street lamps flame
I'd stand alone in James Street
gone...inside my self again.

James Street, the one-time hub of dock life, pulsed with vitality. Tall buildings full of clacking typewriters, clerks, shipbrokers, agents and things maritime. At street level, shops of every degree, elbowing each other for attention. Butchers' windows overflowing with meat and pies, polonies and black puddings, greengrocers with pyramids of Spanish blood oranges, green sprouts, apples and nuts, cake shops, sweet shops, barber shops, chemists—in fact, anything and everything that could be bought or sold was to be found in James Street.

Midway in the centre of this hurly-burly stood the doctor's surgery with its gloomy reception room of fading green and cream emulsion paint. Dominated by a lady receptionist sitting on a Bob Cratchit stool, it consisted of hard wooden benches set around the walls and a solitary table overflowing with ancient magazines, such as *Field and Game, Punch* and *Country Life*. Occasionally, the bell above the surgery door would fail and the patient next in line would be summoned by a muffled shriek from inside. He or she would stumble in for examination, silently genuflecting and followed by the morose looks of the fellow sufferers. A locum, who was said to be fond of a drop of the hard stuff, took over once when the doctor went on holiday. This gentleman never once examined a patient, just listened as he sat behind the desk, grinning from his blotched red face like an inebriated leprechaun. It was said later that the locum cured more minor ailments of Docks folk in a month than the regular GP had done in a year. This was later put down to the law of averages because he had given everyone the same prescription.

Businesses in James Street were as diverse as the customers: Leighton's café, with the free dinners for schoolchildren, another selling a honey-sweet delight called dockers' wedding cake and Brooks, the confectioners of quality. Brooks, with its two aristocratic lady assistants was a nose-on-window for the young locals. Not for Brooks the clutter of lemon drops, not for them the bottles of brandy balls and almond rock. Brooks was the home of bonbons and Turkish Delight with its powdery sugared covering and, best of all—an article of envy that caused many a twitch to small limbs in midnight dreams—large boxes of Nestlés King George the Fifth chocolates in two tiers.

No mention of James Street would be quite complete without some mention of Lane's shop. Mrs Lane, henna-haired and bejewelled, sold just about everything in her small emporium. *Reynolds News, Pegs Paper*, gas mantles and gentlemen's cotton socks at four pence a pair. Like most of the dock's shops, Lane's had its very own aroma: toffee twists and tiger nuts, sherbert dabs and acid drops—this plus a lingering tangy odour that bound them all together and proved to be small square packs of instant fire-lighters.

One surprising feature of James Street was perhaps the dearth of public houses in a district that by today's standards was awash with ale houses. Indeed some small dockland streets boasted more than one tavern, some of which seemed little more than converted dwelling houses. James Street, however, had but three in its entire length, the White Hart, the Ship and the Ship and Pilot, although the last was not known as such. At one time the Ship and Pilot was famed, in particular among the seafaring community, for three well-endowed lady barmaids. And thus the place was ever known as "The Six Tits."

Chapter VI

Holy Days

Corpus Christi

James Street was a happy, bustling place—of shoppers, of seamen carrying sea bags, of the world and his wife and, twice daily, when the bell went in the nearby coal exchange, of stockbrokers, clerks and others who helped swell the throng. James Street's merry march stopped at the swing bridge that stepped over the brown waters of the Glamorganshire Canal. But another, more exciting, march took place annually from a small street not too distant: Corpus Christi, the body of Christ, such a to-do, such a "kerfuffel," when the big day arrived. Tins full of pennies, florins and the odd half-crown that had been secreted away in corners, under floorboards and in dark back-yard sheds had been emptied weeks ago to buy dresses, shoes, blazers and caps.

Saint Cuthbert's Church hall was the scene of a frenzied activity as children were chivvied into line, wrinkled socks pulled up. Schoolmasters rushed back and forth as they mopped at heated bald heads and small girls looked sly-eyed at their neighbours to see who was the better dressed. But when the grand march started it was a brave sight indeed. Led by a drum major with a twirling mace, the band, drums beating and pipes skirling, marched through James Street, West Bute Street and on into Bute Street toward town. The children walked behind, shepherded by a clutch of church dignitaries, teachers and grandmothers in their Sunday best, visibly swelled with the pride of it all as they reached the main street and the awaiting bystanders.

Not an eye turned, not a twitch nor a glance betrayed the marching children, but they saw it all. They saw the cooing womenfolk, they saw the supposedly uninterested menfolk, the sly tongue-poking of jealous small boys and silent weeping of little girls of other faiths who, just for today, wished that they, too, could be Roman Catholics. After marching the broad, asphalted Bute Street—a street that had been denied tramcars and other traffic by large stern policemen—they met marchers from other schools and the whole mighty concourse homed in to the Castle Grounds in a vast testament of faith. It was a day to be remembered, a day to be talked about over cups of tea in back kitchens on dark winter days, a day to be proud of. In short, it was Corpus Christi.

The Saint Patrick's Day dance was another great day in the calendar of Saint Cuthbert's Church. They would be there with the rest, they were the ones whose ancestors had arrived in Wales from Ireland untold generations ago. Yesterday and tomorrow they are as Welsh as a plate of cockles but today, Paddy's day, they are as Irish as a Dublin Bay prawn. They would of course have a drop of the hard stuff before they arrived, to a man sporting bunches of shamrock as big as a navvy's fist in buttonholes or pinned to dresses. And, as the evening and the drinking progressed, so would the Irish brogue thicken, until a stranger would have to pinch himself to make sure that he wasn't in Murphy's Bar in O'Connell Street itself. But that wasn't the end. When the dance was ended some of them would converge on houses in another district to continue the merry-making, to sing wild rebel songs and drink themselves to bed. That was the end of Saint Patrick's Day for another year except for the clink of the chamber-pot under the dark, silent eaves. Tomorrow the roaring, wild Irish Boyo of the night before would become Dai again, as would the heel 'n' toe dancing Bridget become Blodwyn.

Chapter VII

Larboard and the Boat People

The Glamorganshire Canal itself bore a sort of love-hate relationship with local people. On the one hand it was their very own stretch of water, on the other, it was most infuriating to be travelling from one place to another only to find progress halted by a swing bridge that was the very road itself open to allow a sand dredger to pass on up the canal. But the canal was not just a living and thriving waterway, it was a home in every sense of the word to a number of families. Cardiff's own boat people lived in small converted houseboats moored to the canal banks. How they lived is difficult to conceive, their only illumination and warmth on dark winter evenings being a hurricane lamp and blankets. Cooking was on a primus stove or, in warmer weather, a primitive stone-lined hole in the canal bank. None the less, whole families were born, lived and died in this strange watery world.

Other such families prospered in floating homes moored by the Hamadryad Seamen's Hospital and alongside Grangetown's marl. One gentleman who lived by the marl was an all time children's favourite. Rejoicing in the name "Donkey James," he owned a donkey and a small cart with seats. Weekends and summer evenings old Donkey James would hoist squealing, excited children aboard the cart and take them on a guided tour of the docks' shipping, all for a half-penny a ride.

The sand dredgers were perhaps the most loved boats. They would discharge their sand cargo onto the banks of the canal, a cargo that was without doubt a gift from heaven for small and not so small children who had a ready made beach, plus water sports on their doorstep.

Of all the dredgers that discharged sand cargoes on the banks of the canal, perhaps the *Delorain* was the most beloved. It was alongside her sturdy steel side that Docks kids learned to swim. From her decks they learned to dive and it was the *Delorain* which caused small toes to wiggle in delight in Friday school when her steam whistle announced she was in for the weekend stay.

But oh those happy carefree summer days! Who cares a fig for old Barry Island and for the Costa del Sol. It was bread and jam, beef dripping sandwiches, bottles of tap water and, for the very rich, a penny packet of lemonade powder to shake in the bottle. Life was good, life was a game but, best of all, school was a thousand years away. Mothers arrived with broods of neighbouring kids to hear the very latest of local gossip, to get away from steaming kitchens and to take off their shoes and bury their feet in cool silver sand that only yesterday was home to the sand dabs in the Bristol Channel.

The death knell for this wonderful free lido came one

Community swimming pool

evening in the early fifties when the sand dredger, *Catherine Ethel*, smashed into the sea lock. The canal water rushed out to meet its brother, the sea, with a delighted shout, driving the small boat out onto the mud flats and emptying the Glamorganshire Canal for ever. The next morning Docks folk came to view the melancholy sight. Gone was their small stretch of water, gone was the history, the hint of coal and iron barons from the Welsh valleys and the navvies who had dug the cut. In its place lay rusting bicycle frames, parts of old cars, mangles and old Singer sewing machines. But others showed a keen interest in the forlorn and waterless canal. Swarms of treasure hunters, scrap dealers and others descended upon this honeypot, staying for weeks as they pulled and dug in the slimy dross.

An article in the local newspaper spoke of the hunters and how some of them absented themselves from work to lay hands on the booty. Rumours of the finds were rife—of safes full of money, boxes of treasury notes, golden rings, earrings studded with diamonds and, best of all, a whisper of a gold statue that had been purloined from a castle up country. What was found will ever remain a mystery, even down to the statue of gold. When everything of value had been found the scrap dealers turned their attention to the canal banks themselves, removing the very bollards once used to tie up the old canal barges.

Once this final act was fulfilled the authorities decided to fill in the empty space. This was the signal for a different form of bounty hunter to make an appearance. As the army of trucks advanced, tipping stone blocks, chippings and builders' waste into the cut, so the freebooters walked ahead snatching and wrenching valued items in the swirling grey dust like hordes of body snatchers on a deserted battlefield. One man who couldn't believe his luck was Larboard and he was ecstatic. Larboard was the local hermit. An Irishman, he had appeared from nowhere, built himself a shack of old tin sheets and settled in as a bachelor of the parish. Tolerated to a degree by the rough, kindly Docks folk he was someone to pity perhaps and, in many small ways, they looked after him.

It was the rule for Larboard to present himself with an empty tea can at some front door asking for his can to be filled with boiling water, perhaps a pinch of tea—yes a drop of milk would be appreciated, a little sugar, and thank you missis. It was a laugh, a hoot, but people who could ill afford life's little luxuries would feel privileged in a small way that they could help someone in worse circumstances than themselves.

But now this endless stream of lorries, dumping rubble on his own patch, was nothing less than a dream. Larboard moved residence forthwith and built himself a sort of detached villa on the site. He lived there, ate there and slept there. Every evening he would move his shack ready for the next day's proceedings and, as the first lorries arrived come morning, there he was to greet them. Larboard, it seemed, had found fulfilment. Days of knocking on the doors of small terraced houses for a can of hot water and a pinch of tea were in the past. He was now his own man. Every day the loot rolled in from the flock of lorries. He acquired a small drum for a fire, a frying pan and had feasts of bacon rashers, lamb chops and other goodies. He was seen to take a flagon of cider home for a nightcap. Life was becoming a bowl of cherries indeed. He was cleaner. Someone had given him a coat to replace the tattered old mac that had flapped in the wind like a slashed sail. He was a changed man, albeit that he still lived in his detached villa. But he vanished one day, never to return. Rumour had it that he was bitten by a rat one night and was rushed to hospital. Whatever happened, we shall never know, but Larboard went as silently as he had arrived, to leave perhaps just another legend of the docklands.

Chapter VIII

Medicos
and Moonlights

The mighty Coal Exchange building in Mount Stuart Square, north of James Street, still stands square and strong against the four winds. Once the home of merchant princes, its many offices played host to mercantile interests of every degree, including the Shipping Federation. The Federation or Pool was the job centre of the day and at any given time there could be found a couple of dozen seamen seeking situations.

Down the steps beneath the Federation office was "Jackson's Lair," a subterranean medical office presided over by Doctor Jackson, the bespectacled, unsmiling marine medical officer. The office itself, a carbolic smelling dungeon, was bare of furniture except for a small filing cabinet, desk and chair and, in one corner, perhaps for some light relief, a yellowed skeleton, whose half-open mouth leered at visitors like some long dead pirate. The medical examination, although obligatory, was a matter of convenience. Once a seaman had been approved by the Ship Master and the Federation—as long as the man was warm, free of venereal disease and had a reasonable amount of teeth in his head—he was invariably passed A1 and fit for sea service. It was once said that a toothless able seaman, refused medical clearance, borrowed a set of false teeth from a shipmate, returned for a second examination looking somewhat like a shire horse and the good doctor passed him without a second glance. This, of course, is probably a fable, but it adds grist to the time and place.

A few hundred yards on from Mount Stuart Square and its Exchange Building stood an enclave of four narrow streets: Patrick, Hannah, Henry and Alice Streets, now unhappily consigned to history. Patrick Street, with its tall many-roomed houses on the one side, and small terraced houses on the other, was a place to conjure with. Finns, Estonians, Malays, West Indians, Africans, all living together in a glorious humble jumble of humanity.

On one corner was the Cornish Mount, a tavern that was at once a waterhole, club, confessional and palace of varieties rolled into one. The bar, a cosy haven on winter evenings with an open fire roaring up the chimney, had hard wooden benches and chairs and Peter. Peter was the landlady's dog, a canine rascal of indeterminate age and breed who knew every trick in the book and used them to his own advantage.

He was rather partial to a drop of rum, come cold nights, and his ploy for the same would have won him an Oscar in better company. Sitting at a vantage place by the door, he would watch his mistress with the cunning of a jackal. The moment he caught her eye, he would hang his head, give a heart-breaking cough and start shivering as if he was at death's door. It always worked. She would pour a double rum in a saucer, add a drop of water, walk over and place the saucer on the table. Peter was cured in an instant. His shivering stopped. He'd drink his rum, look about him with glee, jump on the bench and lie, legs in the air, snoring for the rest of the night like a drunken bosun.

Considering the small area of the four streets, it bristled with characters, no doubt assisted by the presence of the boarding houses and many bedsits. "Crazy Hans," the Slav "dipso," was ejected by force from every dockside public house for drunken behaviour. There was "Silent Victor," the quiet Estonian, who would walk into a pub and thrust a salt herring wrapped in newspaper into the hot coals of the fire. When the fish was cooked to his satisfaction, he'd remove it, place it on a table and pick delicately at his charred meal over a pot of beer. "Frenchie," the man from Martinique, carried a glass jar containing leeches to be sold for nine pence each to folk suffering from bruises or black eyes. And, of course, there was "Crazy Mac." Mac was a tall, gangling fellow whose legs seemed at constant odds with the rest of his body. Mac's favourite dress in warmer weather was a small cricket cap and a striped blazer of every colour in the rainbow. Mac would, at times, sit in the local pub, singing at the top of his voice, all the while strumming on a guitar that had no strings.

Old "Pop Harris" of Alice Street worked for years at the timber float adjoining the Glamorgan Canal and, although he never once received acknowledgement from any authority, over the years he had rescued dozens and dozens of children from drowning. "Fat Cissy" was another resident of the same street—Cissy of the hundred chins that wobbled every time she laughed, which was often, and probably because she was receiving a marriage allowance from three seamen at the same time. Cissy lived under three aliases, each in the name of one of the three seamen who thought she was his wife. It was a life fraught with danger, but Cissy bore a charmed life; as one man went away so another returned, and the nearest thing to a confrontation came the day that she was wishing one man bon voyage on the London train as another was retrieving his luggage from a coach further on in the same train. But then, nothing ever troubled that jolly, fat lady and she went to her death leaving three grieving sailor men, each one of them mourning the loss of a faithful spouse.

Yet another Alice Street lady, whom it was a privilege to have known, was "Little Edie." Edie, at any given time, was philosopher, historian, raconteur and wit of the highest degree. She had a fund of homespun sayings at her disposal, each starting with "Don't worry. . . ." Her favourite was "Don't worry, as one door shuts another is sure to open." I once heard Edie soothing a young woman whose child kept crying by saying, "Don't worry girl, the more she cries, the less she will pee."

Edie had a hard life in hard times. She was an authority on the art of "the moonlight flit" when a landlord was pressing for rent she never possessed. Her answer to that small problem was to secure other accommodation and then, the evening before the landlord arrived with a final demand, gather her small possessions into a hand cart and fly the coop. Edie was rather proud of the fact that she had done the moonlight flit no less than fourteen times. Sadly the *Guinness Book of Records* was not produced in those days. Whilst Edie had never been quite reduced to complete penury, the wolf ever howled at the corner of the street. None the less, by some means or other, Edie always managed a couple of half-pints of beer in her local.

Perhaps the best moments with little Edie were to sit in her small kitchen on cold nights, the fire spitting, the wind howling about the eaves, and listen to her tales of ghosts, of murders and other crimes as far back as Victorian times. She would tell of the lady in black who, once sighted, meant death in the family, of the white lady who haunted the canal, and of the man who once passed her in Bute Street walking on cloven hooves. Edie would tell these spine-chilling stories until the Westminster chimes of the mantelpiece clock chimed nine o'clock, then she would vanish like one of her ghosts for her drop of ale, leaving her pop-eyed audience shaking in their shoes with fright. Edie and her gritty hard-up thirties friends have long gone, but memory still sees her in that old plaster-flaked kitchen, cooking her sixpenny scrag-end stew, the crowsfeet of age creeping to her eyes as her voice rings back through the year. "Don't worry."

Another small street further on toward the town proper and now vanished with the tread of time was Hodges Row. It included a small row of cottages, a cooperage, an orchard full of peaty leaf smelling soil, later to be prized by folk who took it away in handcarts for their own gardens. But, best of all, an old bus in which children played for hours, driving over imaginary roads and to destinations that only the young know of. Hodges Row, however, was but a stepping-stone to the Bay, the legendary, come day, go day, happy old Tiger Bay.

A thousand yarns have been spun of Tiger Bay and, as the world grows older, more will doubtless be added. Many of the more lurid were whispered by Edwardian agony aunts, who probably never set foot in the place. But one thing is for sure, despite the stories outsiders dreamt up, the safest place for a body to be abroad come the witching hour was, yes, Tiger Bay.

Chapter IX

Bay Ghosts

I first saw the Bay at the end of summer in 1938 sitting, for a little shade, under the trees in Loudoun Square Park. A line of schoolgirls were taking turns to skip inside a rope turned by two of their fellows when one of the girls tumbled, banging her head on the hard concrete. The small crowd gathering in sympathy was pushed to one side by an old woman who, after drying the girl's tears in her pinny, rubbed butter on the bump on her forehead. That was it. The crowd left, satisfied this magic potion was better than any doctor's medicine and the girl, rising to her feet, resumed skipping.

This was Tiger Bay, a place where people had lived together, some for generations, and, no matter their roots, they were all Bay folk. There were hopscotch squares, chalked cricket stumps, gas lamps with bicycle-tyre necklaces and rope-swing scarves, terraced houses leaning together as they looked down on their own scrubbed steps. There were Monday washlines of socks and camisoles, long johns running in the wind, and steamy back kitchens with the copper boiling the whites for the next lineful; but, most of all, there were people.

There were small shops selling this and everything, boarding houses for every nationality, the Universal Men's Home, bath houses in Peel and Angelina Streets, premium clothing cheques, street corner bookies, missions, churches, the crown and anchor and the seven eleven dice . No formal introductions were needed; should you wish to converse with a perfect stranger, that was fine. You heard the cockle man ringing his bell, salt and vinegar to your door, a knife grinder turning his stone and "Fish O!" from Tommy Letton. Tommy was a favourite son. Overcoat swinging open to show a canvas apron as he walked behind his steel-rimmed truck, followed by a grinning army of stalking cats ready to rub arched backs against his leg at every stop. In later years television and radio would farm Tommy's mind for memories of his Bay walks, and a street was named after him in the old man's honour.

The night time Bay shone with yellow light from public houses full of pianos and the windows of the shops. There were sing-songs in the bar, summer concerts from guitars under street lights and the slow walk of Jack and Dai Jones on policeman rounds. Fun there was in plenty. Simple stuff by today's standards but what better than to sit listening to Henry Hall on the wireless, the wind demanding entrance at the back door and the old dog in his corner, twitching in his bone-gnawing, cat-chasing dreams. There was the spark-filled laughter of bonfire night, toasting bread on a long fork as we watched the pictures painted by Sciparti's coal in the

Street life

Zebo black fire grate and dunking heads on Snap Apple night.

Another lilt in the memory is the smell and the taste of the food. Jollof rice with that added touch of cayenne pepper, peas and rice and Tommy Letton's bream with the succulent curry sauce seeping into its bed of rice. Home from the sea and a leg of mutton from Aggie the butcher cooked with slivers of garlic in its basted crinkly sides, roastie potatoes and gravy made in the meat tin, a sight to widen eyes in Bank Holiday glee. Handmade sweets from Canal Zones shop, halva, the honey tasting sweetmeat from the Cairo Café and hot roasted peanuts from the little African, "Peanut Charley." Charley never could find work so he roasted peanuts to help out. When the war started they found him a ship . . . it went to the bottom of the sea with all hands.

There was Gunderson's chip shop in Sophia Street. A warm, steamy home of crisp batter, cod and hake done to a turn, fat chipped potatoes and crimson beetroot. Gunderson's was a dinner-time haven, a child's delight, a place for a quick gossip and a port of call homeward from the "bug house" (the Central Cinema). Public bars flowered in most of the small streets—bars full of conversation and folk with the stumps of pencils in their hands searching the racing columns in the daily papers for a sixpenny double.

Years later, when the bulldozers advanced to tear down the district, I paused to look inside the deserted Westgate Hotel in Angelina Street. It was a broken doll's house. Hanging window frames, the once polished bar covered by the falling ceiling and, over all, the sight of desolation, the smell of rotting wood, leaking gas and tom-cats. Looking at the sad scene, my thoughts echoed into the past, to Mrs Williams' pet parrot marching up and down the bar like a green guardsman, baleful eye cocked for a hand nearing his plate of peanuts. I remembered old Jim Lloyd, flat-capped and sitting in his corner seat, big Rufus elbowing the bar, cigarette dangling from his lips and laughing at one-eyed Johnny, the Liverpool bucko, fresh home from sea and spending his money like water in jolly company . . . . But that was all in the mind's eye, just ghosts flitting through the memory.

Other ghostly happenings had been reported in the Bay since the first sailorman had stepped ashore from his sailing ship. Stories such as the Egyptian ex-seaman returning home to find his wife and child battered to death. Later people would shun the house, come the darkness, because of reports of a woman's figure, candle in hand, as she sat on the stairs of the death house. There was the small, Eton-cropped girl who told her boarding-housekeeper mother of the old lady in strange clothes who had spoken to her in the bedroom of the house. Her mother remembered the story of the old lady whose appearance was said to foretell a death but shrugged the tale off as superstition. Next morning a West Indian boarder fell dead at the breakfast table. In later years two young ladies walking in the dark, deserted streets saw the brother of a friend standing in the doorway of the Peel Hotel. They called greetings but the man never answered; he just stood looking at them in a strange manner. Next day they found that the man they had shouted at had been found dead at the very moment they had seen him.

Children loved these ghost stories, hiding under tables, behind doors and other nooks to listen as grown-ups told them in low voices. Children also loved the Bay, their running, skipping, hop-scotched, comic swapping square mile. They joined the Band of Hope, signed the pledge swearing abstinence for life, screamed delight at magic lantern shows and counted multiplication tables in shrill trebles in Saint Mary's and South Church Street Schools—

Nine twos are eighteen,
Ten twos are twenty!

Whip 'n' top, bonfires, skipping and gobsies, everything had its season, even the white summer return ticket for the tramcar ride to the end of the earth (well, at least Victoria Park) for a penny. The advent of spring always seemed to bring a desire for religious instruction to some of the Bay kids. It was a seasonal holiness, which happened every year and drove them into Sunday schools to sit listening to the gospel in rapt attention like so many plump pickled onions. The reward for this annual show of piety was not just a pat on the head from some misty-eyed Sunday school ma'am, it was the coming Whitsun treat. On the big day girls and boys in starched-frock, short-trousered happiness would board the hired bus or local tradesman's lorry and, with mothers in attendance, ride away shouting and cheering to a local farm for games, races, buns and lemonade. Later, when Whitsun was all over, Sunday school classes would somehow seem much smaller, to the head-scratching wonder of teachers and deacons but, not to worry, as the first green leaves appeared on the Loudoun Square trees, they would all return.

Death, as life, was a shared emotion in the Bay. It started with the laying-out women, called to lay out the dead, place pennies on sightless eyes, a saucer of salt on the stomach and to cover all mirrors with white sheets.

The funeral itself was a public mourning, in essence, with a dignity perhaps not seen in more pretentious districts. Horses, hob-black and plumed in respect, drivers top-hatted and sitting high on a hearse moved slowly in front of soft-footed, two-abreast mourners.

The cortège passed through the blind-windowed street, as sad-faced women and head-bared men looked on, and black-banded sleeves would mark the bereaved for the following twelve months.

But the old Bay has gone, faded into the sea mist which rises each morning over this new Cardiff Bay. Bulldozers were the trumpets for this Jericho until, biblically speaking, not one stone lay atop another. The small streets that once witnessed the pay-offs, the live wires, princes, paupers and the old generation were vacated and stood with front doors clapping in the wind until they too were thrashed into dust.

They built tall flats, shaking hands with the clouds, houses with bathrooms, easy-clean windows, central heating and clothes-lines of steel and plastic that whirled with the wind. They built new shops to replace Jeffries, Lopez, Nicholas, Marshall the bike, Ali Thabit, Aggie the butcher, Tages barber shop and others. Bay girls no longer work in the brush factory, the sack and bag works or Zigmonds; the boys are no longer in foundries or on old tramp steamers.

The agony aunts of yesteryear wrote of grim times, of hard times and, perhaps, in some way they were right. But they never spoke of street parties, Saturday night hops at the Vic and the Premier and, later, the Big Apple and Colonial Club.

Maybe it was grim at times but it wasn't so bad for all that.

Chapter X

Bute Street
Tapestry

Bute Street Thirties

Stalking our past with its memories
like some splendid, exuberant old ghost
Bute Street at night when conditions were right
was Cardiff's own Barbary Coast.

Pawnbrokers, tailors, shipchandlers
grocers and butchers galore
at the end of each day they would close to make way
for the grog shops, the cafés and more.

As evening opened her curtain
and lights flickered on in the bar
the players would start rehearsing a part
for the play in which each was a star.

The barmaids, drunkards, the gentry
sailors ashore for the night
the mate of a tug, old girls in the snug
and wraiths who crept by outta sight.

The Army Salvation and strumpets
brief and licentious affairs
tambourines, bare knees, stockbrokers and thieves
policemen, parading in pairs.

The song of the thirties is over
just a verse in the funnel of time
those extrovert ways, tumultuous gone days
all history, its yours as its mine.

B ute Street bounded helter-skelter from the Pier Head toward the Hayes like a happy tail-wagging dog. This was sailor town: a rolling, swaggering, singing, take it or leave it street, spiced with adventure, the very pavements trodden by seafarers from the four points of the compass.

The Pier Head itself was ever a lonely place given to the four winds and squabbling sea birds and it only came into its own on New Year's Eve. To many Docks folk, the Pier Head was New Year's Eve. Every year, close to the hour, people would gather, sometimes in hundreds, a roaring, kissing, back-slapping, hand-shaking crowd of merry-makers ready to greet the birth of the year, accompanied by a chorus of factory whistles, hooting tugs and ships' Klaxons. Half-an-hour later the place would be deserted as the east wind blew the revellers home to the warmth of their firesides until the next year.

The air at the sea end of Bute Street was painted with the aroma of the Costa Rica Coffee Company, bringing

Happy New Year !

thoughts of coffee cups and toast, oozing butter. Public houses spoke loud of the sea, with their model schooners in glass cases, paintings of steam ships, ship disasters and an occasional ship's bell with spliced bell rope hanging above the bar in readiness to ring stop tap. A small shed that was home to the tram terminus clock stood outside Tony's café with its early morning crew of dockworkers sitting at long tables eating fried bread, tomatoes and ham and eggs. The terminus clock was a staging post for the tram drivers to clock themselves in for the return journey to town, whilst the tram conductor rushed into Tony's café for a refill of tea in his enamelled can. Many a poor conductor, leaving the café, would find a forgetful driver had left without him, starting a mad, tea-slopping rush to catch the tram at the first stop.

Further along the street towards town stood the clothes emporium of "Jones the Goat" and the famed riding mac. Like a statue of Queen Victoria, Big Ben or Nelson's column, the riding mac was an institution. One day a gentleman walked into the shop to purchase the coat, a request so unreal it shook the young assistant, Ben, to his very roots. All was well, however. Closer inspection proved that the riding mac was two-tone: it had stood for so long on display that the sun had bleached the one side of it snow white. Honour was satisfied, the gentleman left empty-handed and the coat was returned to its own special hanger in the window.

Two of the best restaurants in the district—Jack Basani's Popular Café and Pepita's—lay in the small West Bute Street. Pepita's drew many of the theatrical stars appearing in Cardiff theatres for late night suppers. Their limousines were often to be seen outside the café awaiting their owners. Pepita herself had a very fine singing voice, once auditioning for the BBC wireless, no mean feat for the times.

Bute Street railway station, that small gateway to whispered dreams of cockle-filled paddling days in Barry Island, Lavernock Point and St Mary's Well Bay, stood on the opposite side of the street to the George Hotel. The licensee of the George, cloth-capped and quiet, would stand behind the bar awaiting the customers' pleasure whilst his wife, a stout, pleasant woman, sat at a small table outside the bar playing endless games of cribbage. At five minutes to closing time, the landlady would gather together cards and cribbage board, vanish to her quarters until opening time would see her back behind the table ready to resume cribbage battles once more. Rumour had it that the landlord of the George had a secret hoard of money hidden away. This all passed into memory on his death. Later, further rumour spoke of a man who had purchased some furniture from the hotel and, hearing an unusual rattle as he moved a chest of drawers, investigated, finding a small and secret drawer containing twenty-seven golden sovereigns.

A later landlord of the George, dreaming of becoming an entrepreneur, placed a board outside the door showing the time of the next tide plus a notice in large letters, stating:

TIME AND TIDE WAIT FOR NO MAN
COME INSIDE FOR A HOT TODDY
AND A TURKEY ROLL
PRICE 1/6

Trade increased and the landlord, convinced he had a fortune within his grasp, went further, installing a small chip range behind the bar. He employed a young local woman as cook and dressed her in a chef's uniform. The enterprise foundered on opening night. Every time the lady chef opened the cover of the range to serve a sixpenny bag of chips, fat-filled steam flew about the bar killing the froth on pint pots of ale as flat as the sand dabs lying deep in Cardiff Bay.

As with dock roads in most ports of consequence, Bute Street had more than its share of public houses. The

Marquis of Bute, a pleasant family pub on the corner of Hannah Street, was unique among them because of the statue of a man on its roof looking out over the Bristol Channel. During the Second World War blitz, the Marquis of Bute was blown to dust in an air raid and the following morning the neighbourhood was aroused by a woman screaming that she had seen the body of a headless man in the debris. Closer inspection by police and rescue teams found that the body was that of the statue from the roof of the pub, although the head itself was never found. In addition to this, the licensee of the hotel had placed a large amount of money, jewellery and other valuables in the cellar for safety. None of this was ever recovered and presumably still lies deep under the foundations of the Council dwellings now on the site.

Bute Street Norwegian Sailor's Home, built for the needs of the large Scandinavian population living in and sailing from Cardiff, was also a victim of the air blitz. But Cory's Sailors' Mission survived the war to become an auction room and later a furniture store before its eventual demolition.

Of the many Bute Street boarding houses, charging between fifteen shillings and a pound full board, I stayed in two. The first of these was owned by a plump woman from Merthyr Tydfil, who, noting I was a complete stranger, told me Cardiff was a friendly place and I should soon make new friends. She was so right. I met them the very first evening. They were so overjoyed to meet me they near bit me to death. I fled the house at first light and hoped the plump little lady and her bed bugs lived happily ever after.

The second boarding house was unreal, impossible but great fun. Our landlady was a thin, dark-haired Scot of undetermined age who was a great lover of Nestor wine, a grape affectionately called "Red Biddy" and guaranteed to make one as the walking dead if persevered with. She also had a puckish sense of humour, forever telling little jokes and forever forgetting the punch line. It was a pleasure to live in her establishment with one exception, the dreary everyday lunch of vegetable, meatless stew. Her kitchen was a massive dungeon dominated by a large coal-burning stove with an evil-looking aluminium pot on top that she fondly called her stockpot. This pot, the very base of all the vegetable stews, was evidently black death to all salmonella germs. Some of the bones lurking in its depths were doubtless on the hoof when Drake sailed in the *Golden Hind*.

It was an unwritten law that the first one up should light the stove and put the kettle on—a hazard that the wise made note of and stayed abed till it was done by others. The problem was that, should the wind blow from a certain direction, it would blow flame and soot into the kitchen like a small bomb. The landlady once told me she had married a Chinaman who had gone to sea and never returned. I hadn't the heart to say he had probably fled the stove. But for all that, she was a complete charmer and her one hobby (apart from drinking wine) was to attend jumble sales, returning with tailless shirts, odd socks, boots with bunion swellings, and to dole them out to us boarders or "my boys" as she called us.

My most durable memory of her is of the time she heard dark mutterings about the meatless, noonday meals and decided to nip the mutiny in the bud. She called us all into the kitchen, stood there swaying and blessing us with the fumes of Red Biddy, then, with a dramatic gesture, snatched a ladle from a pan boiling on the stove and held it up for us to see, repeating the act time and time again. "See this," she bellowed, "meat every time." Sure enough, every time she lifted that old ladle a lump of meat nestled in it like a little treasure. We left the kitchen chastened and, although we still ate meatless stew every day, not a word was mentioned again. I don't know how the old rascal did that trick but I have a very strong suspicion that she had that lump of meat tied to the ladle.

There were good times, there were lean times. To seamen, who had left home and had no families to fall back on, independence rested solely on the mantle of shipping. On good days we lived high on the hog, on lean days, when shipping was slack and money short, it was a case of "hit the road, Jack," and the boarding houses could offer little succour to penniless rascals with little in view. Once, on the beach as it were, I stayed the night in a stable in Gladstone Street, a small street backing on to Bute Street. The stable's permanent resident, an evil-looking old horse with a turn in one eye, took great umbrage at having his solitude disturbed, and showed his displeasure by glaring over his stall, grinding his teeth and stomping his hooves in a most alarming fashion. All to no avail, I'd walked the dock all day, the straw was warm and sleep came quickly. Dobbin, however, had an ace up his sleeve. Without doubt he had been eating the greenest of grass—that, or he was suffering from extreme gastritis—because periodically he eased his problem by farting like a trumpet. Sleep was quite impossible. As dawn showed his nose through the cracked window, I left in haste, followed by a rousing sailor's farewell from the old villain who was doubtless snorting his head off in victory.

But Bute Street, seasoned by the salt winds from the

Meat stew

Bristol Channel, was not just pubs and boarding houses: it rolled its way toward town, gathering buildings and people like a hen with its chicks. Tea cafés, coffee cafés, the Kardomah, the Cairo, Mr Wing's chop suey, Lavinskys, Copsteins, Lily Volpert's, paper-shops, butchers, the Post Office, chemists, Zussen's pawnshop, grocers, the Police Station—you name it, you got it, and all under the benevolent eye of the twin towers of St Mary's Church.

Access to Zussen's pawnshop was through a small door, flanked on the one side by a Zussen's merchant navy outfitters, on the other by Zussen's jewellery and knick-knack shop. The pledge room was basic. Chocolate-brown paint, fading cream distempered walls, a lonely light-bulb guarded by a celluloid collar and a porridge-grey counter from behind which an assistant sprang at the very first tinkle of the shop bell. The assistant, a melancholy creature, who merged with the gloomy atmosphere, had a voice honed on a gravestone and long, bony fingers that wandered over any article to be pledged like inquisitive spiders. More to this, he knew every trick in the book and was blessed with a variety of facial expressions, ranging from incredulity to downright horror, if asked for a half-penny more than the value of the article to be pawned. Zussens took most things. Bed clothes, shoes, men's suits, jewellery, watches—pawned on Monday, redeemed on Friday. In Zussen's book, if it was moveable it was hockable and it was a sad day for many when the shop closed.

Gone too are those wonderful old buildings and the characters who helped weave the tapestry of Bute Street and the docklands. But pause awhile some quiet autumn evening and listen. You may hear the voices of the men from the valleys who filled the taverns with song on rugby nights. Look closely into the shadows—is that some old seaman with his donkey's breakfast on his shoulders as he staggers a little on the way to join his ship, or is it even "Scotch Nelly" grinning into her glass of Red Biddy? Walk with the seabirds as they argue over the same crusts at the Pier Head. You may hear the faint echo of New Year revellers, catch a taste of coffee from the Costa Rica Company or a thought of riggers, dock workers and coal trimmers.

Some day a better pen than mine will fill many of the gaps left by this small history. But, until then, that's how I saw it.

Old Tiger Bay

Old Tiger Bay, old Tiger Bay,
I treasure your memory in every known way
those two-storeyed houses with front doors ajar
the sound of a piano from each jolly bar.

A canvas of life in a terraced square mile
where neighbours made time to converse for a while
boarding house, café, a sly gambling den
seamen and dockers . . . Revenue men.

Street vendors and hawkers, who'd stopped by your door
with paraffin, cockles, oilcloth for the floor.
the corner shop chippy, a sixpenny treat
as noses on window, kids watch from the street.

Outsiders viewed your name in alarm
but they knew not the pleasure, the fun and the charm
of the boys on the corner on a warm summer's night
strumming guitars 'neath the mellow lamplight.

Of weddings, street parties, the girls starched and clean,
and the little old ladies in their best bombazine.
the bookies, the packmen, the haves and have nots,
dancing the polka in humanity's plot.

Nostalgia grows stronger as day follows day,
for the vanished mystique . . . that was old Tiger Bay.

Rainbow's End

If I could find the rainbow's end
and taste Dame Fortune's kiss
I'd ask she wave a magic wand
and grant me just one wish.

That I could have a cabin'd boat
close by the harbour mouth
and when the wayward wind blew fair
I'd set my course due south.

A passing gull as sailing mate
my chart the evening sky
we'd sail back into memory
a nomad boat and I.

To pull aside the drapes of time
a fool to some it seems
whose thoughts are cloistered in the past
with half forgotten dreams.

Of laughing seas, of hurricanes
and sprinkled harbour lights
and sailing down some spice filled coast
on jasmine scented nights.

The boatman's song in Calabar
the palms in Port-au-Spain
and rusted ships who round the Horn
to dance in doldrum rain.

Pacific waves on coral reefs
the sound of soft guitars
on islands lazing in the sun
like strings of sleeping stars.

Then when the salt washed journey's run
I'd come back home to stay
and seek out new tomorrows
that live in yesterday.

Remembering